The Bookworm Mystery

TEEN READERS
TR
TEEN READERS

About the Author

George Ivanoff was born in Melbourne, Australia on 12th February 1968. He got married in 1999 and has two children. He graduated from the National Theatre Drama School, but also has a BA (Hons) and an MA in Australian Studies. He is both a writer and an actor.

He has written over 60 books and short stories for children and teenagers as well as magazine articles and anthologies. His Gamers' series, Gamers' Quest (2009) and Gamers' Challenge (2011), are very popular in Australia. It is a science fiction series about Tark and Zyra who live in a world of magic and science.

He has also appeared in a number of short films, feature films and television and theatrical productions.

George Ivanoff

The Bookworm Mystery

TEEN READERS · TR · TEEN READERS

George Ivanoff
The Bookworm Mystery
Teen Readers, level 2

Illustrations: Birgitte Frier Stewart

Edited by: Joanne Popp
Series editor: Charlotte Bistrup

ISBN Denmark 978-87-23-90800-1
www.easyreaders.eu

Easy Readers
EGMONT

Printed in Denmark

Chapter 1

Partners

"Russell and Jessica."

"No," *sighed* Rusty, as he put his head on the table.

"Is there a problem, Russell?" asked the teacher.

"No, Ms Conyers," Rusty answered, without looking up.

Joint projects were bad enough, thought Rusty, but a joint project with a girl who loved sport and never got higher than a 'C' was a *nightmare*. In the end, he'd do all the work – he just knew it. But at least that way he'd get an 'A'. Rusty was certain that if Jessica did any of the work they would get a 'C'. He always got an 'A' in history. He didn't want that to change.

All the class now had a partner, Ms Conyers' class was over and Rusty didn't move. He had his head down on his table, and was still thinking about how *unfair* the situation was.

"Are you *sick* or something?" asked a voice. "Or just a *weirdo*?"

Rusty looked up at a very *freckled* face, with a lot of orange hair on top.

"I'm fine," he lied.

---

to sigh [saɪ] to breathe out loudly when you are not happy
joint [dʒɔɪnt] when two or more people do something together
nightmare ['naɪtmeə] bad dream
unfair [ʌn'feə] when something doesn't feel right
sick unwell; ill
weirdo ['wɪədəʊ] someone who is strange
freckled ['frekəld] see illustration on page 8/9

"Hello, Fine," said the girl with the freckled face. "I'm Jess."

"Huh?"

"It's OK," sighed Jess, *shaking* her head. She sat down on the chair next to Rusty. "So where do we start, *Bookworm*?"

"Huh?"

"I thought you were supposed to be *brainy*," said Jess. "The project!"

Jess waited for him to say something more but he didn't. "Well ... I think we should start at the school *library*."

Rusty looked out of the window and still didn't say anything.

"We could go right now," suggested Jess. "It's Friday. I haven't got any *hockey* practice today."

"No!" Rusty shouted. Then a *smile* came across his face. "I know a better place."

hockey

---

to shake – shook [ʃʊk] – shaken to move from side to side
bookworm someone who reads a lot of books
brainy ['breɪni] knowing a lot; clever
library ['laɪbrəri] place where you can borrow books
smile, to smile your mouth does this when you are happy, see illustration on page 8/9

Chapter 2

The Library

“Is this it?” asked Jess, you could hear the *disappointment* in her voice.

“Well, what were you expecting?”

“But it’s just another library,” *complained* Jess, as she looked at the old building. “And it’s really old looking.”

“It’s old,” *agreed* Rusty. “But that’s what is so good about it. It’s got a lot of really old books.”

“So?”

“We’re doing a project about local history,” explained Rusty. “So old books are what we need. And this library has a whole section of books about this town and its people.”

“How do you know all this?”

“Because I come here every day after school,” said Rusty.

“Why?” she asked.

“I want to read every book in this library,” he explained. “So I’ve got to work at it every day.”

“Really?” Jess looked at Rusty as if he wasn’t normal.

“It’s my special *goal*.”

Jess smiled. “Like a hockey goal?”

---

disappointment [ˌdɪsə'pɔɪntmənt] the feeling when something isn’t as you hope it will be

to complain [kəm'pleɪn] to say that something isn’t how it should be

to agree [ə'griː] to think the same as someone else

goal [gəʊl] 1. Doing a difficult task or job; 2. A place where you have to put the ball to get points in a team game like football

freckled
bookshelf
newspaper

smile
sign
MORTON TOV
LOCAL HISTO
filing cabinet
librarian
desk
Morton Daily
drawer
dress

Rusty just looked at Jess concerned. Then he saw her little smile.

"You're *joking* … right?" he asked.

Jess *nodded*. "You're quick, Bookworm."

"Come on," said Rusty, opening the door. "And stop calling me Bookworm."

Rusty led the way into the old building.

The *librarian* at the front *desk* nodded and gave Rusty a smile as they walked in. Jess thought that she looked too young to be a librarian. And her *dress* was too short. Librarians are old and *boring*, aren't they?

"Hi, Mrs C," *whispered* Rusty.

He led the way through the main part of the library, where there were a lot of *bookshelves* and computers. Then they walked through the open study area, which was full of whispering students sitting at large tables with books in front of them. At the back of the library there were four bookshelves full of books, three *filing cabinets* and a small table with two chairs. There was a *sign* on the wall above the filing cabinets: MORTON TOWN LOCAL HISTORY.

"This is it," said Rusty.

"Yeah," said Jess. "Great."

"Now what?"

"Now we start the research."

---

to joke to say something funny

to nod to move your head up and down

librarian [laɪˈbreəriən], *desk, dress, bookshelf, filing* [ˈfaɪlɪŋ] *cabinet, sign* [saɪn] see illustration on page 8/9

boring [ˈbɔːrɪŋ] the opposite of 'interesting'

to whisper [ˈwɪspə] to say something quietly

"Yeah, but what are we looking for? We don't know what our project is about yet. I thought we were just going to get a book about our town and choose a chapter. I didn't think there was going to be this much to read. I thought this was going to be ..." Her voice *trailed off*.

"Easy?" Rusty asked.

"Well ... yeah," agreed Jess.

"Getting A's isn't easy," said Rusty, as he walked to the first of the bookshelves. He started to look through the books.

"I don't get A's," said Jess.

"Really?" Rusty said to himself.

"So where do we start, Boo--?" Jess asked.

"Just look around," said Rusty so Jess couldn't finish. He took a book off the bookshelf and started looking at it. "See if anything looks *interesting*."

Jess looked from one bookshelf to another. There seemed to be so many books. She didn't know where to start. Then her eyes went to the filing cabinets. Now that was something she knew about. Her mum worked in an office, and in the last school holidays Jess had gone to work with her mum to help with some *filing*.

She went over to the first filing cabinet and pulled open the top *drawer*. It was full of *folders*. She pulled one out. Cindy Beresford 1937-2001, was written on it. The picture

---

to trail [treɪl] *off* to stop speaking in the middle of a sentence
interesting the opposite of 'boring'
to file to sort out papers and put them away
drawer [drɔː] see illustration on page 8/9
folder you put papers in it to keep them together

showed a woman with black hair and big eyes. She looked very serious. She was the town's first woman *mayor*. The folder had a lot of stories from *newspapers* in it. Boring!

Jess tried another folder: Gordon Brakowitz 1899-1952. He was a *sad-looking* man with black hair and a *pale* face. He wrote *poems* and had written the town poem. Jess didn't know the town had a poem. The folder had many poems in it, a lot of pieces cut out of newspapers and also a list of books. Jess didn't like poems, so she quickly put the folder back in the drawer.

She closed it and tried the second filing cabinet. More folders. More boring people! She moved to the last filing cabinet and pulled the top drawer. As the drawer opened, the filing cabinet fell forward.

Jess got out of the way quickly as the filing cabinet fell over with a big bang.

Rusty stood still, he couldn't move. Then he came running over. "What happened?"

"Oh no, what's happened?" said a voice from behind. They saw the librarian coming towards them.

"Are you both OK?" she asked.

"Yeah," nodded Jess. "I opened the drawer and the filing cabinet fell over."

---

mayor [meə] the person who organizes things in a town
newspaper see illustration on page 8/9
sad-looking not looking very happy
pale almost white, without much colour
poem ['pəʊɪm] lines of text that usually rhyme

"That filing cabinet is *empty*," explained the librarian. "No one has used it for years. It's supposed to be *locked* so that people don't open it." She said and walked back to her desk.

"I never thought history could be *dangerous*," said Jess.

"What's that?" asked Rusty, looking at something on the back of the filing cabinet. Jess reached down, and pulled off an old *envelope*. On the front were the words:

Look and you shall find.

"Should we open it?" whispered Jess.

"Yes," said Rusty, quietly.

Jess opened the envelope and pulled out a piece of paper. "A letter!" she said.

"A *mystery*!" whispered Rusty, looking at the letter.

envelope ['envələʊp]

address [ə'dres]

---

empty ['empti] the opposite of 'full'
locked ['lɒkt] can only be opened with a key
dangerous ['deɪndʒərəs] the opposite of 'safe'
mystery ['mɪstəri] something which you cannot understand; secret

CHAPTER 3

The Letter

March 25, 1980
To the person who finds this letter ...
Good day to you!

Many people claim life to be a mystery. Perhaps that is why we are pulled towards the smaller mysteries within our lives.
Now you have the opportunity to solve a mystery. The first step was finding this letter. The question is: will you take the next step? To solve the mystery is to find a treasure. Thus to begin, the Bard can help you.

Good luck,
Edgar Morganstein III

Rusty and Jess looked at the letter.

"It's some sort of *joke*," said Jess. "Isn't it?"

Rusty shook his head. "I don't think so. The envelope and letter are old and a bit yellow. They have been here a long time."

treasure ['treʒə]

to solve to find the answer to a problem
joke a funny story

"Well, if this is real," said Jess, "there might be some treasure at the end, if we solve the mystery?"

"Perhaps," agreed Rusty.

Jess put the letter on the table. "So who's this Edgar man?"

"I don't know," said Rusty, looking up at the bookshelves. "Perhaps he's in one of the books."

"Or perhaps he's in the filing cabinets."

Jess went over to the second filing cabinet and opened the first drawer.

"M's are in here," she said, looking through the files. "I've found him!" The picture was of a man with brown hair, brown eyes and a *beard*. There was a lot of information in the folder. It said that Edgar had a lot of money. He was also a book *collector* and liked old and *rare* books. He had given money to the library so they could start their rare books *collection*. He died on March 26, 1980, when his car went off the road, into the sea. His body was never found. He had no *relatives*, so his money went to various museums, libraries and *charities*.

"See," said Jess. "The man had a lot of money. So there's probably some treasure just waiting to be found!"

"Perhaps," said Rusty, looking at the letter again.

"So," said Jess. "If we do our project on this man … finding the treasure can be part of the research. But where do we start?"

"'Hamlet'!" said Rusty, suddenly. "We start with 'Hamlet'."

beard [bɪəd]

collector someone who has lots of similar things
rare [reə] not seen or found very often
collection a lot of things that are similar and special
relative [ˈrelətɪv] your aunt, uncle, sister, brother, cousin, etc.
charity [ˈtʃærɪti] organization which gives people money or help if they need it

Chapter 4

'Hamlet'

"What do you mean?" asked Jess.

"The letter says, the Bard can help you," explained Rusty. "The Bard. That's William Shakespeare."

"I see," said Jess, in a voice that made it obvious she didn't really see.

"Now look at the letter," continued Rusty, *excitedly*. "Can you see how some of the letters look different? They're *darker* than the others. Let's put all the dark letters together: H-A-M-L-E-T. 'Hamlet' is one of Shakespeare's most *famous* books."

Jess didn't know who Shakespeare or Hamlet were. "So ..."

"We need to look at 'Hamlet' for a *clue*." said Rusty. He was walking up and down and talking to himself. "But which book? There are so many." Suddenly he stopped. "We need a really old one. That's it! The rare books collection."

He looked at Jess, who was still looking at him with her mouth open.

"Don't you see?" he said a bit *annoyed*. "Morganstein

---

excited [ɪk'saɪtɪd] happy about something
dark this is when there is no light
famous ['feɪməs] someone or something that everyone knows
clue [klu:] piece of information that helps you find the answer
annoyed [ə'nɔɪd] unhappy about something

liked old and rare books. He gave his money to this library to start a rare books collection. There's going to be an old *copy* of 'Hamlet' in that collection."

Rusty ran to the front desk and Jess ran behind him. The librarian was on the phone, talking to someone about the filing cabinet.

"Mrs C?" asked Rusty. "Can we go into the rare books collection?"

Mrs C looked at Rusty while still talking on the phone. She reached under the desk and took out a book and a pen. She gave them to Rusty and he wrote the time and his name. Then he gave the pen to Jess and she wrote her name, too.

"Thanks," he said, and then he showed Jess the rare books collection. There were about five really high bookshelves full of books. There was also a computer and a large table with four chairs.

Rusty went to the computer and *typed* in 'Hamlet'.

"The library has 12 copies of 'Hamlet'," he said. "Two of them are in here."

He went to the right bookshelf and got the two books. He took them to the reading table and gave one to Jess.

"Here. You look in that one, and I'll look in this one."

Rusty opened his copy. He slowly looked at each page.

After a few minutes, Jess asked: "Um ... what am I looking for?"

---

copy ['kɒpi] here: one single book from a large series of books
to type [taɪp] to write on a computer

"I don't know," said Rusty, without looking up. "Something!"

After another few minutes, Jess said, "Well ... I think I've found ... something."

Rusty looked up. She had the book open at the first page.

She *pointed* to something written on the inside of the front of the book.

Given to the
Rare Books Collection
by Edgar Morganstein III
on March 25, 1980

"That's just before he died," said Rusty, excitedly. "And it's the date on the letter."

He started looking through the pages, one by one. It took a long time. Jess was just getting bored, when he said, "Ah-ha!"

"What?" asked Jess.

"Look at this," said Rusty, showing Jess the book. One line had been *underlined* in pencil.

To be, or not to be: that is the question.

"Yeah," said Jess. "What does that mean?"

---

to point [pɔɪnt] to use your finger to show someone something
to underline [ˌʌndəˈlaɪn] to draw a line under something

"It's where Hamlet, the Prince of Denmark, is thinking about *committing suicide.*" Rusty looked up at Jess. "Perhaps Morganstein committed suicide and didn't have a car *accident*?"

"Why would a man with that much money want to kill himself?"

"Who knows," said Rusty. "But if you have money you aren't always happy."

"So how does the underlined bit help us?" Jess asked.

"I don't know," said Rusty. "Perhaps there are more clues in the book."

He continued looking through the pages, until he reached the end. There, on the inside of the back of the book, was more writing.

To see a World in a ***grain*** *of sand,*
And a ***Heaven*** *in a wild flower,*
Hold ***Infinity*** *in the* ***palm*** *of your hand,*
And ***Eternity*** *in an hour.*

"Hmm," whispered Rusty. "Interesting."

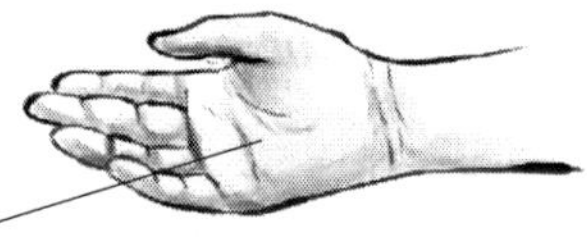

palm [pɑːm]

---

to commit suicide [ˈsuːɪsaɪd] to kill yourself
accident [ˈæksɪdənt] something bad that happens and which you can't stop
grain [greɪn] small piece of something
heaven [ˈhevən] place where you go when you die
infinity [ɪnˈfɪnɪti] never ending distance or time
eternity [ɪˈtɜːnɪti] time that doesn't end

Chapter 5

Poems and Things

"What's interesting?" asked Jess. "What does all that mean?"

"It's from a famous poem by William Blake. It's interesting because it's about *enjoying* life. It's completely *opposite* to the underlined bit in 'Hamlet'."

"But is it a clue?" asked Jess.

"Oh, yes," said Rusty. "It's a clue. And I know where to go next."

He ran to the computer, then to one of the bookshelves, and then back to the table, carrying a book: 'The Poems of William Blake'.

"I don't like poems," said Jess.

"What if they help us to find the treasure?" asked Rusty.

He put the book on the table and opened it. There was writing on the inside, the same as in 'Hamlet'.

"Was it given on the same day?" asked Jess.

Rusty nodded. He then *turned* to a page in the book. He found the same lines, underlined in pencil, that were written in the back of Hamlet.

"We've found the right book, again," said Rusty.

"Go to the back of the book," said Jess, excitedly. "See what it says."

---

to enjoy [ɪnˈdʒɔɪ] to like doing something
opposite 'wrong' is the opposite of 'right'
to turn [tɜːn] to move to the next page or in another direction

Rusty went to the last page of the book. This time there was nothing written there.

"Did you think it would be that easy?" whispered Rusty.

"I was *hoping* it would be," sighed Jess.

"Things are never that easy."

Rusty looked at the page with the underlined text again. "Umm ...," he whispered to himself, as he looked through the pages. "Blake wrote another similar poem."

He turned the pages of the book and found the poem he was looking for. There was something written on the left of the poem. This time it was telling them to look at Herman Melville's 'Moby Dick'.

And so it went on for the next hour, each book telling them to look in the next one. The clues were getting more and more difficult. Then they came to an Australian *atlas*. This one had also been given to the library by Morganstein on March 25th 1980. There was writing next to the *map* of their town. It read: *tome emporium*

(25 × 9) ÷ (5 × 5)

spectre

"So is this another clue to another book?" asked Jess, who was really getting annoyed. Where was the X? Didn't all hidden treasure have an X to *mark* the *spot*?

"I don't think this one is quite that simple," said Rusty.

"So what is it?" asked Jess.

"I don't know."

atlas ['ætləs]

map

to hope [həʊp] to want or wish something good will happen
to mark to show where something is
spot place on a map where something is

Chapter 6

Tome Emporium

"It's written in an atlas … so … I think it must be a clue to a place."

"A place?"

"Yes," said Rusty, smiling. "I think it's an *address*."

"I don't understand," said Jess.

"The first line," said Rusty. "Tome is another word for book. And emporium is another word for shop. So tome emporium means bookshop."

"So this is the address of a bookshop," said Jess.

"Yes. And the second line is the street number. Twenty-five times (x) nine is … um … two hundred and twenty-five. Five times five is twenty-five. And 225 divided by (÷) 25 is … hold on … 9."

"So is spectre the name of the street?" Jess asked.

Rusty nodded. "I think so. Let's look in a street map."

They went to a different part of the library and found a street map. But there was no Spectre Street in their town.

"Maybe this bookshop's in the city," said Jess. "Or even another state."

"Or," said Rusty. "Spectre is not the name of the street, but a clue to the name."

---

address [ə'dres] see vignette on page 13

Rusty smiled, took the street map and looked through it. Then he showed the book to Jess and pointed at Eidolon Avenue.

"I don't understand," said Jess.

"Spectre and eidolon are both other words for *ghost*," explained Rusty.

"Oh." whispered Jess to herself.

"We have to go to the bookshop at 9 Eidolon Avenue," said Rusty.

"Well, we'd better be quick," said Jess. "My mum doesn't know where I am."

They were out of the library and on their bikes within minutes. Jess could have got to the bookshop in less than ten minutes, but Rusty was so slow.

When they got to Eidolon Avenue Jess stopped outside the shop and got off her bike. Rusty got there a minute later.

It was a small shop with a window full of books. It was called 'Rose and Eddy's *Pre*-loved Books'.

"This has got to be it," said Rusty. "Eddy – as in Edgar Morganstein III."

They left their bikes on the *pavement* and went inside.

It was a dark shop with too many bookshelves in it. Every bookshelf was full of books. There were also *piles* of books between the bookshelves. Next to the door was a little desk, with piles of books on it and a *cash register*.

ghost ['gəʊst]

---

pre- before or earlier

pavement ['peɪvmənt], *pile, cash register* ['redʒɪstə]
see illustration on page 26/27

"Wow!" sighed Rusty. "This is so cool!"

"It is?" said Jess.

"We're closed," said a voice from behind one of the bookshelves.

"But we've come about Edgar Morganstein III," said Jess.

An *elderly woman* put her head out. She had grey hair and *glasses.*

"What?"

"Edgar Morganstein III," said Jess, again.

"*Key* ... words," whispered the old woman.

"Huh?" said Jess.

"Keywords," *repeated* the woman, her voice now strong.

"Keywords?" asked Rusty.

The old woman looked down at the *floor* and sighed. "Words are the key to understanding."

"I don't understand," said Jess.

"We're closed," said the woman again, and went back behind her bookshelf.

"We just wanted to ask a few questions," said Rusty.

"Get out," called the voice.

As Rusty and Jess went out of the shop, the old woman looked out from a pile of books. She watched them as the door closed.

"That's it," said Jess. "I give up."

"We can't give up," said Rusty.

---

elderly ['eldəli] *woman, glasses, floor* [flɔːː] see illustration on page 26/27
key [kiː] see illustration on page 30/31
to repeat [rɪ'piːt] to say something again

“Watch me,” said Jess, getting on her bike.

“But what about the project?” asked Rusty. “What about the treasure?” he shouted after her.

But Jess went.

floor

elderly woman
pavement
cash register
glasses
pile

Chapter 7

The *Furniture* Shop

Rusty slowly ate his toast. It was Saturday morning and he was still thinking about the day before. How he had got the clue wrong and how Jess had left him.

"Is everything OK?" asked his dad.

"Yeah," said Rusty.

"Really?" said his dad.

Rusty nodded and put some more toast in his mouth.

Beep ... beep ... beep! Rusty took out his mobile phone. He looked at the *text message*:

Meet u @ library. 10am. Got addy.

Rusty started to *choke* on his toast.

"Jess!" he *spluttered*.

"Oh, yes," said his dad. "And who's Jess?"

"Project partner," said Rusty, as he started *texting* back.

"Uh-huh," said his dad, with a smile on his face. "Just a project partner? Not a girlfriend."

Rusty's face went red. "No!" he said. "Got to go."

Rusty's dad *laughed* as his son left.

---

furniture ['fɜːnɪtʃə] chairs, tables, cupboards
text message a short message you send on your mobile phone
to choke [tʃəʊk] to have difficulty breathing or eating
to splutter ['splʌtə] to make sharp noises when breathing and trying to swallow at the same time
to text to write a message on your mobile phone
to laugh [lɑːf] you do this when someone says something funny

It took Rusty ten minutes to ride his bike to the library.

Jess was already there.

"I know the address," she told him. "You said spectre was another word for ghost. Well ... there's a Ghost Gum Street. And it's about five streets that way." She said pointing.

"Why are we waiting?" asked Rusty, happy that Jess was still thinking about the project.

"You," laughed Jess. "Come on."

Jess got on her bike and was off. Rusty followed her quickly. Within a few minutes they were standing in front of a shop called 'Handmade Furniture'.

"Furniture?" said Rusty.

Jess looked down annoyed. "I was wrong."

"Wait and see," said Rusty. "Perhaps we should take a look inside."

Rusty tried to open the door but it was locked.

"It's OK," said Jess. "It's a furniture shop, not a bookshop."

"It used to be," said a voice from behind.

There was a man behind Rusty and Jess. He was wearing old jeans and a T-shirt, and had some keys in his hand.

"It used to be called the 'The Old Book Emporium', many years ago," explained the man. He put one of the keys in the door. "There are still a few books in the back room."

"Great!" said Jess, excitedly. "I'm right after all."

"Can we look, please?" asked Rusty. "We're doing a school project about local history."

The man opened the door and stood to one side. "Go in and look."

storeroom
corner

workshop
frame
box
key

They went through to a back room that was full of furniture and *boxes*.

"I use this as my *storeroom*," said the man. "But in that back *corner* are a few piles of books that were left here when I bought the shop. You can have them if you like."

"Thanks," said Rusty.

"I'll leave you to it. I've got a cupboard to finish. I'll be in the *workshop* if you need me."

Rusty and Jess started to look through the books. There weren't many of them, but it took them almost an hour to look through them for clues.

"I give up," said Jess. She closed the book she was looking at and sat down next to a box.

"Again?" asked Rusty. "Hey, what's that?"

As Jess had sat down, a box on the floor had moved. There was something on the wall.

"There's a picture or something on the wall behind the box," said Rusty.

Jess looked behind her. The two of them then moved the box out of the way.

They both smiled. It was a picture of Edgar Morganstein III standing outside 'The Old Book Emporium'.

"That's it," said Rusty. "The next clue."

Jess took the picture off the wall and looked on the back of it.

"There's nothing written on it," she said.

"That would be too easy," said Rusty. "It's probably inside the *frame*."

---

box, storeroom, corner, workshop, frame see illustration on page 30/31

Slowly, he took the *clips* off the frame. He took off the back and then took out the picture. There was nothing written on the back of it.

Rusty put the frame back together and put it back on the wall.

"The clue must be *somewhere* else around here," he said. "We've got to keep looking."

"What if the clue was taken with the books when the shop closed?" asked Jess.

"It must be still here ... somewhere."

"If only pictures could talk," said Jess, looking at Edgar Morganstein III. "Wait a minute!" Jess looked at the picture again. "The picture **is** telling us something. Look!" She showed it to Rusty.

Rusty looked at the picture. Then he smiled. "Hey, you're getting good at this!"

Jess smiled and *blushed*.

In the picture, Edgar Morganstein III was holding a book. It was called 'Rare Books and Where to Find Them'.

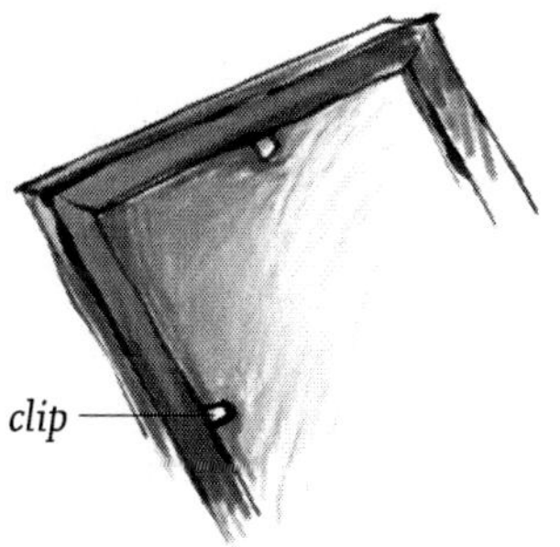

---

somewhere describes a place you don't know about
to blush [blʌʃ] to go red when someone says something

Chapter 8

'Rare Books and Where to Find Them'

Rusty and Jess *raced* into the library. They went to the nearest computer and looked for 'Rare Books and Where to Find Them', but the library didn't have a copy.

"There must be a copy around somewhere," said Jess. "It's the clue."

"There's an easy way to find out," said Rusty, looking at the computer.

Within *seconds*, they were looking at the town's museum on the Internet. 'Rare Books and Where to Find Them' was written by Edgar Morganstein III. He had *published* the book himself. There were only 50 copies *printed*, which Morganstein had given to his book collector friends. The museum actually had Morganstein's own copy. He had given it to the museum on March 25, 1980.

"That's the same day he gave the other books to the library," said Jess.

"It **must** have the next clue in it," said Rusty.

"Come on, let's go." said Jess excitedly.

They got on their bikes and were quickly at the

---

to race to run fast
second there are 60 of them in a minute
to publish ['pʌblɪʃ] to make a book and sell it
to print to produce writing or pictures on the pages of a book

museum. After buying their *tickets*, they went through the different rooms to the rare books section. There, behind *glass*, on a special bookshelf were three books. There was an old copy of the Bible. A copy of 'Our Town', which was the first book ever published in Morton Town, in 1898. And Morganstein's copy of 'Rare Books and Where to Find Them'. The book was open at the first page, where Morganstein's name was written in the top corner.

"It looks like the same writing as all the other clues," said Rusty.

"So the mystery really is from Morganstein," said Jess.

Rusty put his hands on the glass and looked at the book. "But how do we get to look inside it when it's behind glass?"

"We could ask," said Jess.

"They'll never let us," said Rusty.

"Come on," said Jess, going to the front desk.

"Can we look through 'Rare Books and Where to Find Them', please? It's in the rare books section." She said to the woman at the front desk.

The woman looked at them for a few seconds, pushed her glasses up her nose and then she started laughing.

"You kids are always joking around."

"Um ... we're not joking," said Jess, looking serious. "We need to look at it for a school project on local history."

The woman stopped laughing. "Oh, no," she said, seriously. "No one is allowed to read the books in the rare books section."

"But they're books," said Rusty. "They're meant to be read."

---

ticket, glass see illustration on page 36/37

glass
ticket

bald
suit
bow tie
EXIT
security guard
29
Rare Books and Where to Find Them
uvenir
Rare Books and Where to Find Them
Buy your copy here

"They are **rare** books," said the woman. "They need to be *protected*."

"The library has rare books," answered Jess. "And we're allowed to read them."

"Here you can't," she said. "It's against the rules. You can't *touch* that book. No one can."

"But –" started Jess.

"But," said the woman, stopping her. "Copies are available in the museum shop. You could always buy one."

Rusty smiled. "Great!"

"Thanks," said Jess.

"You're welcome," said the woman. "Now go or I'll call a *security guard*."

"What?" Rusty and Jess looked at the woman.

"Got you!" she laughed.

Rusty and Jess smiled, thanked her again, and went to the museum shop.

The shop had postcards and *souvenirs*. Near the door was a small pile of books. 'Rare Books and Where to Find Them' was on the top of the pile. Rusty read the back:

This book was written by the book collector Edgar Morganstein III. Morganstein's personal copy of 'Rare Books and Where to Find Them', is now kept in the Morton Museum Rare Books Section. It has been printed again for the first time.

---

protected [prəˈtektɪd] safe from danger
to touch [tʌtʃ] put your fingers on something
security guard [sɪˈkjʊərəti ˌɡɑːd], *souvenir* [ˌsuːvəˈnɪə] see illustration on page 36/37

Within these pages you will find the original book and also Morganstein's written ***notes*** *from his own copy.*

You have to have this book if you are a collector of rare books or a student of local history.

"This is it," said Rusty. "Now we can read it!"

"You have to buy it to read it," said the man at the desk. He was big, with a *bald* head and a long nose. He was wearing a grey, *suit* with a black *bow tie*. And he looked annoyed.

"OK, we'll buy it," said Jess.

"That will be $59.95."

"Oh," said Jess.

"Oh," said the man. "Now if you put the book back ..."

"But we're doing a school project about Edgar Morganstein III," explained Rusty. "We need to look inside this book."

"Well, then you'll have to buy it."

"But we haven't got the money," said Rusty.

"Then you have to find something else to write about."

"Couldn't we just –"

"No!" And he turned his back on them.

---

notes things you write quickly so you don't forget them

bald [bɔːld], *suit* [suːt], *bow tie* [ˌbəʊ ˈtaɪ] see illustration on page 36/37

Chapter 9

Ms Conyers

Rusty and Jess slowly left the museum shop.

"That man is …" started Jess.

"Teacher!" said Rusty, stopping her.

"No. That's not what I was going to say."

"Teacher," said Rusty again, pointing.

Ms Conyers was standing at the museum door. She saw Rusty and Jess, *waved* to them and walked towards them.

"Are you working on your project?" she asked.

"Yeah," said Jess. "Well … we were."

"We've got a problem," explained Rusty.

"Really?" said Ms Conyers. "Tell me about it."

"We're doing our project on Edgar Morganstein III," said Rusty.

"He was a book collector," said Jess.

"Yes, I know," said Ms Conyers. "He was an interesting man – he is a good idea for your project. What's the problem?"

"The problem is his book, 'Rare Books and Where to Find Them'," said Rusty. "We've found everything else we need."

"Yeah," agreed Jess. "We've looked at the information in the local history section in the library. And we've looked at the books he gave the library."

---

to wave to move your hand in the air

"But we haven't been able to find a copy of 'Rare Books and Where to Find Them'."

"Yeah," agreed Jess, again. "We need to read it. But the library doesn't have a copy."

"The only copy is in this museum," said Rusty.

"And it's behind glass," said Jess. "So we can't read it."

"The museum shop is selling copies," said Rusty.

"But the man in the shop won't let us read it if we don't buy it," said Jess.

"And we don't have $59,95," said Rusty.

"So we can't go on," explained Jess.

"But you seem to be working together well," said Ms Conyers. "I knew you'd make good partners. Now, about the book – I've been meaning to buy a copy for the school library. I could buy it today and let you read it over the *weekend*, but you have to bring it to school on Monday."

"We *promise*!" said Rusty and Jess together.

"Well, then," said Ms Conyers, "come with me."

She took them into the museum shop and bought a copy of the book.

"Happy reading," she said, giving it to Rusty.

The man behind the desk looked at Jess and she just smiled back at him.

"Thanks, Ms Conyers," said Rusty.

---

weekend Saturday and Sunday
to promise to tell someone you are going to do something

Chapter 10

Keywords

Rusty and Jess waited until they were in the town library before they looked at the book. It seemed like the right place to read it.

Rusty slowly opened the book and started looking through the pages.

"Wow!" sighed Jess. "He made a lot of notes."

It seemed like Morganstein had written on every bit of white on every page.

"This is going to take weeks," said Rusty.

"How do we find out which notes are the next clue?" asked Jess.

"I don't even know where to start," answered Rusty.

"Start at the beginning," said Jess, slowly. "Start with the first clue. That Ham book by that Bard man."

"'Hamlet'?" said Rusty, nodding. "Let's try."

Rusty looked up 'Hamlet' in the back of the book. Then he went to page 98. There was a section about 'Hamlet'. At the top of the page, Morganstein had written, 'Rose and Eddy's Pre-loved Books'.

Jess pointed to the page. "That's the bookshop with the *weird* old woman."

---

weird [wɪəd] very strange or odd

Rusty nodded. Then he pointed to another note written at the *bottom* of the page.

To be, or not to be: that is the question.

"Isn't that the underlined bit in the 'Hamlet' book?" asked Jess.

"Yes," answered Rusty. "But look."

Rusty pointed to the first two words. Under each of them, Morganstein had drawn a little key.

"The keywords," whispered Jess.

Rusty nodded.

"That means we need to go back to that bookshop," said Jess. "And give the weird woman the keywords."

"It means a lot more than that," whispered Rusty, looking up at Jess. "It means that Edgar Morganstein III did not die in that car accident."

"What?"

"'To be or not to be'," said Rusty, excitedly. "To live or to die. He chose to be – to live. I don't think he died!"

---

bottom the opposite of 'top'

CHAPTER 11

Rose and Eddy

"They never found his body," said Rusty, as he and Jess got off their bikes.

"So ... what? Do you think he *faked* his own death?"

"Well, why not?" Rusty asked. "People have done it before. To get away from things like not very happy lives."

"Oh, yeah," said Jess. "If I had a lot of money I'd be faking my own death."

"Come on," said Rusty, as he opened the door to 'Rose and Eddy's Pre-loved Books'.

"Just a minute," called a voice, as the little *bell* rang when Rusty and Jess opened the door.

The weird woman made her way between the bookshelves, carrying a *huge* pile of books. She couldn't really see where she was going. She got to the front desk and put her books on another pile that was already there. She looked up and saw Rusty and Jess.

"Oh, you're back," she said. "So ... what do you have to say this time?"

"To be," said Rusty.

The woman *staggered* back and sat in the chair behind the desk. "W-What?"

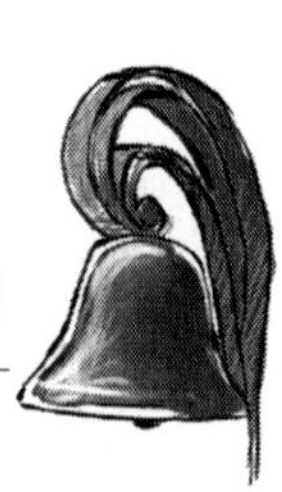

bell

to fake to pretend
huge [hju:dʒ] very, very big
to stagger ['stægə] to walk in a funny way as if carrying a heavy weight

"To be," repeated Rusty. "The keywords."

"We followed Edgar Morganstein's clues," said Jess, excitedly.

"Well, I'll be," whispered the woman. "I didn't think anyone would ever do it."

"Well, we have," said Jess, very happy with herself. "Now, what's the treasure?"

"Treasure?" smiled the woman. "The best treasure there is – knowledge."

"What?" said Jess, she wasn't very happy.

"Cool!" said Rusty.

"Oh, there is so much to tell you," said the woman. "But first, I think we need some *tea*."

She got up, locked the front door and turned the little sign around to CLOSED. Then she took them into the back room. There was a small kitchen with a table covered in books, four chairs and piles of books on the floor.

"By the way," said the woman, "my name is Rose."

"And the Eddy is Edgar Morganstein III," said Rusty.

"My, my, my, you really have worked it all out, haven't you?" said Rose, as she started to make the tea.

"So he isn't dead!" said Rusty. "He faked it."

"Yes," said Rose, with a sad-looking face. "He did fake his death at the time. But death gets us all in the end."

She stopped making the tea and looked at Rusty. "You're a little late. Edgar died about six months ago."

Rose finished making the tea in *silence*. She brought three cups to the table and sat down.

---

tea [tiː] hot drink that is very popular with English people
silence [ˈsaɪləns] period of time when there are no sounds

"Now," she said. "Edgar's life wasn't everything you may think it was. He had a lot of money but he wasn't happy. All he wanted was a simple life.

Rose drank her tea. "And there were always people who wanted to be his friends, because of who he was, when it was really his money that they wanted. I think I was his only true friend. He wanted to stop working and just do what he really wanted to do – have a quiet little bookshop. Books were what he loved most in life. Books ... and mysteries ... book mysteries. Games, really. We used to play them all the time – ever since we were kids. He'd write clues, leading from book to book, and I'd try to solve them. I never was very good at it. Bookworm mysteries – that's what I used to call them."

Rose *paused* to drink more tea. "He saw that he'd never really be able to stop working. People just wouldn't let him. He thought that the only way out would be to die. Or, at least, to make people think that he had died. And Edgar being Edgar ... well ... he just had to leave some clues and make it all a mystery."

"So there is no treasure," said Jess.

"I'm not really sure," said Rose. "I know that Edgar wanted to do something special if anyone ever solved the mystery and found him. But I don't know what. You'll just have to be happy with the knowledge you've found."

"Well, I'm happy," said Rusty. "I'm happy we solved the mystery. I'm happy that we've got a school project out of it. And I'm happy that Mr Morganstein didn't die in the car accident and that he lived a happy life."

---

to pause [pɔ:z] to stop doing something for a short time

Rusty started to drink his tea, and then remembered why he didn't usually drink tea – because it was YUCK! He put the cup down and moved it across the table.

"Why didn't he live to see you two solve his biggest bookworm mystery?" said Rose. "I'm sure he would have been very happy. I wish there was a treasure I could give you." Rose finished her cup of tea. "It's funny … Edgar died in his sleep. When I found him in the morning, he was holding a copy of Robert Louis Stevenson's 'Treasure Island'."

Jess's eyes opened wide. "You don't suppose …"

"What?" said Rusty. "That he started another mystery? Just before he really died?"

"Well …" said Rose, thinking. "It would be a very Edgar thing to do." She got to her feet. "Wait a moment." She went over to a pile of books in the corner of the room. "I'm sure that his copy of 'Treasure Island' is here somewhere." She started looking through the books. "Ah-ha!"

She brought an old copy of the book to the table and put it in front of Rusty and Jess. On the front, the word, 'Treasure' had been underlined in pencil.

Rusty picked up the book and looked through some of the pages. He whispered, "One letter has been underlined on each page."

"Yes!" said Jess excitedly. "It's another mystery!"

"Oh, my," said Rose. "What does it spell?"

"Well, let's find out," smiled Rusty. "The first letter is …"

Comprehension and activities

Before you read this book

Look at the picture on the front of the book and the title.

a) What do you think this book is going to be about?
b) Who do you think the main people in the book are?
c) What made you choose this book to read?

Chapter 1
Partners

Questions on the text

a) Why did Rusty put his head on the table?
b) Why doesn't he want to do the project with Jess?
c) Is Jess happy that she is doing the project with Rusty? What makes you think this?
d) Have you ever had to do a project with someone you didn't like? Did you work well together?
e) Where do you think 'the better place' is that Rusty wants to go to?

Chapter 2
The Library

Questions on the text

a) What did Jess think of the library? What is the library like in your town?
b) What does Jess think about Rusty going to the library every day and his goal?
c) Did Jess and Rusty have an idea for the project?
d) Do you think Morton is a big town? What makes you think this?
e) Would you have taken the envelope or would you have given it to the librarian?
f) What do you think is written in the letter?

Chapter 3
The letter

Questions on the text

a) Who wrote the letter?
b) What sort of letter is it? If you found a letter like this would you believe it? Would you follow the clues? Why / Why not?
c) Where did Jess and Rusty find information about the letter writer? Where would you look for more information about someone? List a few ideas.
d) Do you think there is any treasure at the end of the mystery? If so, what do you think it could be?

Chapter 4
'Hamlet'

Questions on the text

a) Who is the 'Bard'? What more do you know about him?
b) What was the first clue in the letter?
c) What did Jess and Rusty have to do before they could go to the rare books collection in the library?
d) What did Rusty do when they got to the rare books collection in the library?
e) Who found the first thing that was useful? What was it?
f) Which line was underlined in 'Hamlet'?
g) Why do you think Rusty thought the writing in the back of the book was interesting?

Chapter 5
Poems and things

Questions on the text

a) Which book did Jess and Rusty need for the second clue?
b) What does Jess think of poems? What do you think of poems? Why?
c) Was the next clue in the same place in this book as the last clue? Where was it?
d) What were Jess's feelings after spending over an hour in the library without finding any treasure? How would you have felt? Would you have given up looking?
e) What do you think the clue in the atlas is telling them?

Chapter 6

Tome Emporium

Questions on the text

a) What other words mean ghost? Name two that are in 'The Bookworm Mystery'. What others do you know?
b) Why do Jess and Rusty have to be quick?
c) How did they get to the shop? Who got there first, Jess or Rusty? Why?
d) What sort of shop was it?
e) What was the woman like in the shop? Describe her without reading the chapter again, then check if you were right. Add any information you missed.
f) Why wasn't Jess happy when they left the shop?

Chapter 7

The Furniture Shop

Questions on the text

a) What did Jess mean in her text message when she wrote: Got addy.?
b) What was Rusty doing when the text message came?
c) How did his dad make him feel when he said who the text message was from? Why do you think he felt like this?
d) What sort of shop was in Ghost Gum Street? What sort of shop did it used to be?
e) Where was the next clue? How did Jess and Rusty find it?
f) Where do you think Jess and Rusty are going to look next?

Chapter 8
'Rare Books and Where to Find Them'

Questions on the text

a) Where did Jess and Rusty find the book 'Rare Books and Where to Find Them'?
b) How did they find out where the book was?
c) Why couldn't they look at the book?
d) Where can people buy a copy of the book? Why couldn't Jess and Rusty buy one?
e) Describe the man who wouldn't let them look in the book.

Chapter 9
Ms Conyers

Questions on the text

a) How did Jess and Rusty solve the problem of buying the book?
b) Did they tell Ms Conyers about the mystery and the treasure they were looking for? Why? Would you have told your teacher?
c) What did Ms Conyers think of Jess and Rusty's project and how they were working together? Was she surprised?
d) What did the man in the shop think when Ms Conyers bought the book?

Chapter 10
Keywords

Questions on the text

a) Why do you think Jess and Rusty thought the library was the right place to read the book by Edgar Morgenstein?
b) What did they decide to do so that they could find the next clue?
c) What are the two keywords?
d) Where do Rusty and Jess have to go and what do they have to do there?
e) What did Rusty think the keywords meant? What do you think they meant?

Chapter 11
Rose and Eddy

Questions on the text

a) How did the woman in the shop feel when she saw Jess and Rusty again?
b) How did the woman in the shop react when they told her the keywords?
c) Why was Edgar Morgenstein not happy with his life?
d) What did he like doing and what did he want to do?
e) What was the treasure at the end of 'The Bookworm Mystery'?
f) Do you think Jess and Rusty started solving the clues for the new mystery? What would you have done?

a) Were you right? Was the story about what you thought it was going to be about?
b) What would you have changed in the story to make it better?
c) Did you like the ending? Do you want to know which word the letters spell?
d) Write another chapter for 'The Bookworm Mystery' with your ideas about how the story could carry on.

Find more exercises on
www.easyreaders.eu

Teen Reader Titles Now Available

English

Level 0

Philip Hewitt: Emma and the Boy Next Door (Sound)
Ann Halam: The Shadow on the Stairs

Level 1

Peter Johnson: Runaway Teacher
Alan Posener: The Double Life of a Very Black Cat
Stephen Speight: Bed & Breakfast (Sound)
Stephen Speight: The Runaway
Jeremy Taylor: Dr Schnitzler´s Dog
Jeremy Taylor: All 4 Love (Sound)
Wolf/Ferro: The Missing Mascot (Sound)

Level 2

Rita Bennet: The Scary Chat Room (Sound)
Kevin Brooks: Johnny Delgado – Private Detective
Annie Dalton: Friday Forever
Paul Davenport: Horror Trip on the Pecos River (Sound)
James Heneghan: Hit Squad
James Heneghan & Norma Charles: Bank Job
Philip Hewitt: Helping Hands
Philip Hewitt: Terror in the Hills
George Ivanoff: The Bookworm Mystery
Karen Mccombie: Love is the Drug
E. E. Richardsson: Black Bones
E. E. Richardsson: Devil for Sale (Sound)
Stephen Speight: The Fjord Murder (Sound)
Stephen Speight: Summer School Adventures
Andy Stanton: Sterling and the Canary
Jeremy Strong: Mad Iris
Jeremy Taylor: Football Friends (Sound)
Jeremy Taylor: Luke (Sound)
Lee Weatherly: Them

Level 3

Anne Cassidy: Talking to Strangers
Paul Davenport: A Matter of Principle
Paul Davenport: Crossroads to Love (Sound)
Paul Davenport: Wolf Watch
Paul Davenport: Snakeman
Charles Ferro: Horror at Remsen High
Charles Ferro: Moonstruck
Charles Ferro: Love Ties
Charles Ferro: Burning Love
Charles Ferro: The Fortune Teller
Charles Ferro: Kool-1
Charles Ferro: The Cave Mystery
Charles Ferro: Vampire Skeletons
Charles Ferro: Voodoo Zombies
Philip Hewitt: Quest for a Father
Sylvia Olsen: Yellow Line
Alan Posener: Oh! Carol and Other Steve Stories
Jeremy Taylor: Love me Blindly
Tony Varrato: Fakie

Level 4

Charles Ferro: Forever Young
Charles Ferro: Over the Line
Holly-Jane Rahlens: One Fine Day

German

Level 0

Iris Felter: Mädchen & Der Junge am Meer (Sound)
Greta Gallandy: Keine Angst? (Sound)
Patricia Mennen: Kopftuch

Level 1

Iris Felter: Tanz mit mir!
Greta Gallandy: Im Chatroom gefangen
Alan Posener: Kater, Ines und Katerina

Level 2

Alan Posener: Märchenland
Elsegret Ruge: Vier Freunde - Abenteuer in München (Sound)

Level 3

Alan Posener: Olli aus Ossiland

French

Level 0

Laurent Jouvet: Radio mystère (Sound)
Christiane Stéfanopoli:
Catastrophe au Camping des Roses (Sound)

Level 1

Michel Amelin: Cent vingt minutes pour mourir
Pascal Garnier: Les enfants de la nuit (Sound)
Lenia Major: La lettre mystérieuse
Brigitte Peskine: Mon grand petit frère (Sound)
Jérôme Talou: Parce que je t'aime

Level 2

Stéphane Daniel: Un agent trés secret
Anna Gavalda: 35 kilo d'espoir
Charlotte Gingras: Un été de Jade
Laurent Jouvet: Anne et l'ordinateur (Sound)
Laurent Jouvet: Répétition pour un crime
Jérôme Talou: L'amour par internet (Sound)
Paul Thiès: Un automne rouge sang (Sound)

Level 3

Michaël Ollivier: Frères de sang
Jérôme Talou: Bruno et l'amour

Level 4

Hallum/Louveau: Choc des cultures

Spanish

Level 0

Jaime Corpas: Amigos virtuales
Javier Navarro: Un mundo fantástico

Level 1

Jaime Corpas: Misterio en la Sagrada Familia
Javier Navarro: Una historia de montaña

Level 2

Javier Navarro: Las estátuas de Machu Picchu

Sound: Available as either Mp3 or CD,
check www.easyreaders.eu

Teen Reader Titles Now Available

Read On Series
English
Level 2 (A2) - including CD

Benni Bødker: Sarin in Sulphur Valley
Benni Bødker: Sarin in the Emperor's City
Benni Bødker: Sarin in the Foggy Mountains
Benni Bødker: Sarin in Nordheim
Benni Bødker: Sarin in the Salt Mine
Benni Bødker: Sarin and the star Tower

A-team Series
– Free mp3 available at www.easyreaders.eu
Level 3

Daniel Zimakoff & Ida-Marie Rendtorff: The Computer Mystery
Daniel Zimakoff & Ida-Marie Rendtorff: The Stolen Monkey
Daniel Zimakoff & Ida-Marie Rendtorff: Kidnapped

Labyrinth Series
German
Level 3 (A2/B1)

Martina Gattermann: Ein dramatischer Urlaub
(Sound available)
Martina Gattermann: SOS aus Wien
(Sound available)
Martina Gattermann: Horror in Hintertux
Martina Gattermann: Abenteuer in Berlin